Will Rogers

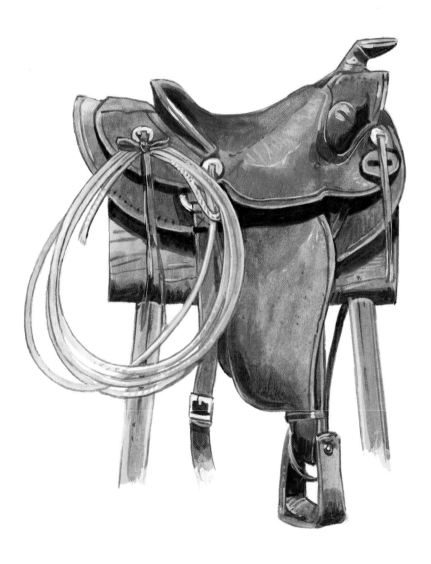

Will Rogers

by Jane A. Schott
with illustrations by
David Charles Brandon

Carolrhoda Books, Inc./Minneapolis

To my mother, who has always encouraged her children to be readers.

—J.A.S.

To my father, Arthur Brandon, who introduced me to the writings of Will Rogers.

—D.C.B.

The photograph on page 44 appears courtesy of the Will Rogers Memorial, Claremore, Oklahoma.

This book is available in two editions:
Library binding by Carolrhoda Books, Inc.
Soft cover by First Avenue Editions
c/o The Lerner Group
241 First Avenue North, Minneapolis, MN 55401

Library of Congress Cataloging-in-Publication Data

Schott, Jane A., 1946–
   Will Rogers / by Jane A. Schott ; with illustrations by David Charles Brandon.
      p.   cm.
   ISBN 0-87614-983-2 (lib. bdg.)
   ISBN 1-57505-030-7 (pbk.)
   1. Rogers, Will, 1879–1935—Juvenile literature. 2. Entertainers—United States—Biography—Juvenile literature. 3. Humorists, American—Biography—Juvenile literature. I. Brandon, Dave, 1942–. II. Title.
PN2287.R74S36 1996
792.7'028'092—dc20
[B]   95-43434

Manufactured in the United States of America
1 2 3 4 5 6 – S – 01 00 99 98 97 96

Indian Territory, 1884

Willie sat on the top board
of the corral fence.
The sun was burning high in the sky.
Dust was swirling.
Flies were buzzing.
But five-year-old Willie Rogers
didn't move.

He heard the calves calling
for their mothers.
He saw a cowboy heating
branding irons at a fire.
He smelled burning hair.
And he watched Dan Walker,
the best cowboy on the ranch.

Dan threw the lasso again.

It fell quickly over the head of a calf.

Dan pulled the lasso hard and tight.

The calf jumped and pulled.

When the branding iron came down,

the calf yelped.

Then Dan loosened the rope,

and the calf skipped away.

Over and over, Dan threw the lasso.

Willie never saw him miss.

Not once.

Willie's fingers itched to throw a lasso, too.

He could do it.

He knew he could!

More than anything,

Willie wanted to be a cowboy.

Willie was born in 1879.

He lived on his parents' ranch
in Indian Territory on land
that later became Oklahoma.

Willie and his parents were part
Cherokee Indian.

Like most of his family and friends,
Willie grew up with cowboys and cattle.

And he loved it.

Willie practiced throwing a rope
the way Dan did.
He watched other cowboys rope, too.
And then he practiced some more.
After what seemed like a very long time,
Willie could rope a fence post.
But he wanted to do more
than just rope fences.

One day, Willie asked Dan
to show him some tricks.
Dan showed Willie different ways
to twirl a rope.
He showed him the right way to hold
his hand and arm while throwing.
And he told Willie
he would have to practice *a lot*.

That was fine with Willie.
There was nothing he liked more
than roping.
Later, some people said Will Rogers
must have been born with a rope
in his hand.
He made it look so easy.
But then, he'd been practicing
just about all his life.

After Willie learned to rope,
he roped *all* the time!
Sometimes at night,
he dreamed about roping.
"Catch him! Catch him! Rope him!
Don't let him get away!" he called out
in his sleep.

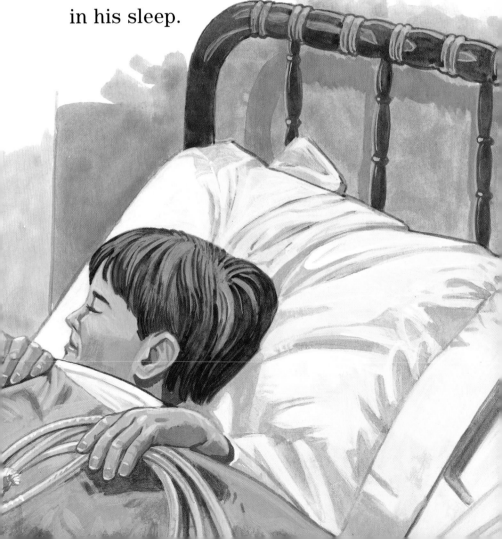

When Willie was six years old,
his father gave him a pony.
Riding his pony,
Willie felt like a real cowboy.

But Willie couldn't be a cowboy
all the time.
He had to go to school.
And he didn't much like it.
Often he would sit staring out
the school windows.

Willie wasn't supposed to take
his rope to school.
Sometimes he took it anyway.
At recess, he would rope
the other children
just to make them laugh.
The teachers didn't think
Willie's tricks were so funny.
Willie's father sent him to a lot
of different schools.
He hoped Willie would settle down.
But at every new school,
Willie got in trouble again.

Finally, Willie's father sent him
to a military school.
Willie was told *not*
to take his ropes with him.
But he tied them around his bags,
and no one even noticed.

After getting in trouble again,
Willie decided he couldn't stand
school any longer.
He was eighteen years old.
And he would call himself *Will*, not Willie.
He was ready to be a real cowboy.
Will knew his father would not want
him to leave school.
So he didn't go back home.
Instead, he found a job
on a ranch in Texas.

A Real Cowboy

Will pulled his bandanna up
over his nose and mouth.
The herd of cattle
was kicking up clouds of dust.
Being a cowboy was hot, dusty work.
But Will loved this cattle drive.
Finally, he was a real cowboy!

All day long, he rode across
the wide prairies.
He moved his horse in and out
of the herd.
He had to keep the cattle going
in the right direction.
He had to make sure they found good
grass to eat and clean water to drink.

At night, he slept under the stars.
He was so tired he never felt
the little rocks under his blanket.

Each morning, the cook made coffee,
biscuits, and beans over the campfire.
The other cowboys laughed at how much
food Will could put away.
All the hard work and fresh air
made Will so hungry!

When that cattle drive was over,
Will found some other jobs.
But it was getting harder and harder
for a cowboy to find work.
Towns were growing larger.
Workers were laying train tracks
across the wide grasslands.
The prairies were slowly
being fenced in.

After one cattle drive,
Will went back home.
He tried raising cattle of his own.
He even bought a new pony,
named Comanche.
But Will wasn't really happy.
What he liked best was
the cowboy life of roping and riding.

Then one day, Will heard about
a steer-roping contest.
That's what he needed!
Will practiced his roping and riding
harder than ever.
On the day of the contest,
Will was riding Comanche.
All around him,
people were laughing and talking.
But Will kept his eyes on the cattle chute.
Suddenly a steer ran down the chute.
"Go!" called a voice.

Will rode Comanche toward the steer.
He threw his lasso neatly
over the steer's horns.

Will told Comanche to stay put.
Jumping down, he grabbed the front leg
and the back leg of the steer.
Then he quickly tied them together.

The people cheered.

Will Rogers won first prize.

That day changed his life forever.

Will knew it was going to be hard to
find another job as a cowboy.

Now he wondered if people would pay
to see his roping and riding tricks.

New York City

Will Rogers walked onto
the New York City stage.
All at once, people stopped talking.
Who was this man dressed
in cowboy clothes?
Would he sing or dance or tell jokes?
Will was a little scared.
But the feel of the rope in his hands
helped calm him down.

Suddenly a horse and rider came out
from behind the curtain.
Will was ready.
The ropes flew through the air.
Not one lasso, but two!
One dropped around the horse's neck.
The other pulled tight
around the rider's chest.

Will took a bow and
waited for people to cheer.
This trick was very, very hard.
Will expected people
to clap loudly and yell.
Maybe even whistle.
But they only clapped politely.
Will was disappointed.

Later, a friend talked to Will.
He said that people did not know
how hard the trick was.
The next night, Will told
the crowd about his trick.
"I don't have any idea I'll get it,"
he told them, "but here goes."

This time, when he roped
the horse and rider,
people clapped and laughed.
At first, Will was angry.
Why were people laughing at him?
Then he thought about it some more.
They were laughing because
they liked his tricks—and his talk.

Because Will's tricks were so hard,
he sometimes missed.
When the lasso would not
go over the horse's head,
he would grin.
Then he would say,
"Think I will turn him around
and see if I can't throw one
on his tail easier."
Once, when nothing
was going right, Will said,
"Out West where I come from
they won't let me play with this rope.
They think I might hurt myself."
Sometimes people laughed
more when Will missed a trick
than when he got it right.

In 1916, Will was hired to work
in the *Ziegfeld Follies,*
the most famous stage show
in New York City.
People came to shows to laugh
and forget their problems.
Will Rogers, the talking cowboy,
was just what they needed.
He would start twirling his rope,
watching it rise and fall.
Then Will would tell a joke
in his friendly cowboy way.
When he looked at the crowd,
his eyes seemed to say,
"Did you get it?"

Will was in the *Follies*

two times every night.

It kept him busy thinking up jokes.

He said, "I like one where

if you are with a friend,

and hear it, it makes you think,

and you nudge your friend and say,

'He's right about that.'"

Most nights, Will told jokes about

things he read in newspapers.

On other nights,

he talked about himself.

Sometimes, Will bragged about

being Cherokee.

He said, "My ancestors may not have

come over on the *Mayflower*,

but they met 'em at the boat."

Bigger and bigger crowds
came to see and hear Will Rogers.
He was becoming very famous.
As a boy, he had dreamed
of being a cowboy.
He had practiced long and hard
to become one.

Now he knew he had something
more important to do.
There were millions of Americans
who needed to laugh.
Will Rogers was just the cowboy
to help them do it.

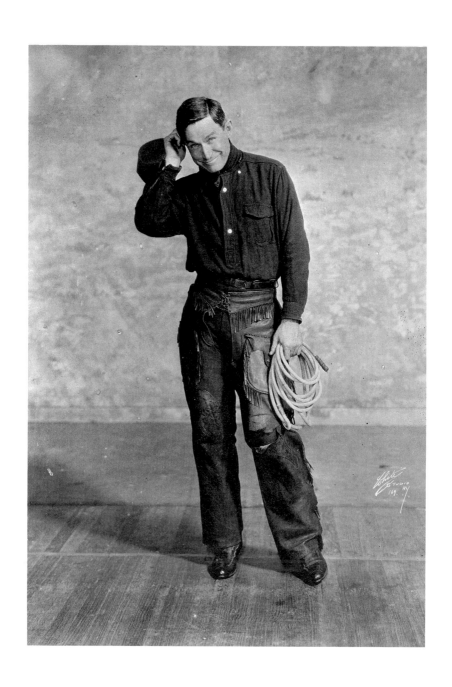

44

Afterword

In 1908, Will Rogers married Betty Blake. Later, Will would say, "The day I roped Betty, I did the star performance of my life." They had four children—Will Junior, Mary Amelia, James Blake, and Fred Stone Rogers.

Will left the *Ziegfeld Follies* in 1919. He went on to become a star of movies and radio. He wrote six books and a daily newspaper column. And although Will became famous, he never forgot his Cherokee heritage or the land he grew up on in Oklahoma.

Will was killed in a plane crash near Point Barrow, Alaska, in 1935. He was 55 years old.

Americans and other people around the world were shocked to hear of his death. It was hard for them to believe that Will Rogers would never be on stage again. Everyone would miss the friendly cowboy. President Franklin D. Roosevelt spoke for all Americans when he wrote, "Will Rogers . . . showed us all how to laugh."

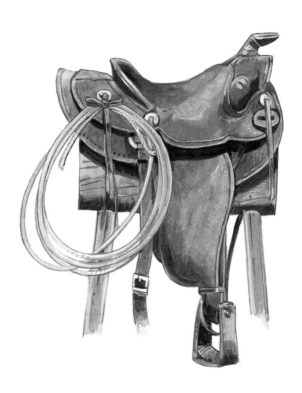

Important Dates

November 4, 1879—William Penn Adair Rogers is born on a ranch in Indian Territory near what is now Claremore, Oklahoma.

1890—Mary America Rogers, Will's mother, dies.

1897—Will's father, Clem Rogers, sends Will to Kemper Military School.

1898—Will gets his first job as a cowboy on a cattle drive from Higgins, Texas, to Medicine Lodge, Kansas.

1905—Will goes on the stage for the first time in New York City.

1908—Will marries Betty Blake on November 25.

1916—Will joins the *Ziegfeld Follies*.

1919—Will moves to California and makes silent movies.

1922—Will writes his first newspaper column.

1929—Will makes his first "talkie" movie.

1933—Will begins his weekly radio show.

1935—Will is killed in a plane crash in Alaska.

1938—The Will Rogers Museum and Library open near Claremore, Oklahoma.

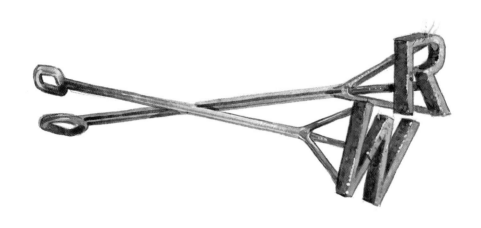

New Words

branding iron: a tool that is heated and used to mark cattle to show who owns them

cattle drive: a way of moving cattle from one place to another, usually over a long distance

chute: a path with fencing on both sides

corral: a pen built of fencing to hold animals

cowboy: a person who works for a ranch tending cattle

lasso: a long rope with a loop at one end, made for throwing over the heads of animals

prairie: wide-open land covered with grass and few trees

ranch: a very large farm used for raising large numbers of animals

steer: a male of the cattle family, raised for beef